SWU-NAP- 008

UNIFORMS OF RUSSIAN ARMY DURING THE NAPOLEONIC WAR VOL.3

UNDER THE REIGN OF PAUL I
EMPEROR OF RUSSIA BETWEEN 1796 AND 1801
THE CAVALRY

From the Viskovatov's greatest work:
"Historical description of the clothing and
arms of the Russian Army"

English translation by Mark Conrad

SOLDIERSHOP PUBLISHING

AUTHOR

Aleksandr Vasilevich Viskovatov born 22 April (4 May New Style) 1804, died 27 February (11 March) 1858 in St. Petersburg, Russian military historian. He graduated from the 1st Cadet Corps and served in the artillery, the hydrographic depot of the Naval Ministry, and then in the Department of Military Educational Institutions. He mainly studied historical artifacts and the histories of military units. Viskovatov's greatest work was the Historical Description of the Clothing and Arms of the Russian Army.

TRANSLATOR

Mark Conrad is an American historian with a great interest for all the Russian history.

Title: **UNIFORMS OF RUSSIAN ARMY DURING THE NAPOLEONIC WAR VOL. 3 - The Cavalry**
By A.V.Viskovatov. English translation by Mark Conrad. First edition by Soldiershop.
Cover & Art Design: Luca S. Cristini. Plates re-colorations by Anna Cristini
ISBN code: 978-88-93270533

Published by Soldiershop publishing, via Padre Davide, 7 - 24050 Zanica (BG) ITALY. www.soldiershop.com

UNIFORMS
OF THE RUSSIAN
ARMY DURING THE
NAPOLEONIC WAR VOL.3

UNDER THE REIGN OF PAUL I EMPEROR OF
RUSSIA BETWEEN 1796 AND 1801

*

The Cavalry

Nach der Natur gezeichnet durch Thomas Weber in Augsburg 1799.

Fr. Vogel fec.

Kaiserl. Rußische
Cürassier - Dragoner - Hußaren

HISTORICAL DESCRIPTION OF THE CLOTHING AND ARMS
OF THE RUSSIAN ARMY - A.V. VISKOVATOV
(First English translation by Mark Conrad)

Soldiershop is glad to presents the complete collection of the great job made by A.V. Viskovatov dedicated to the uniforms and weapons belonging to the Russian army during the Napoleonic period, until 1825. The time we considered corresponds to the reigns of two Tzars: Paul I, who reigned since 1769 until his murder on the 23rd of March 1801, and his son Aleksandr Pavlovi□ Romanov, that with the title of Alexander I, sat on the throne until the 1st December 1825.

Our reprint in based on the original 19th century volumes, to be precise the volumes from 7 to 9 are dedicated to the reign of Paul I; this first part is distributed on 7 volumes, having a numbering from 1 to 7. From number 10 to 18 of the original volumes, the second part is dedicated to the Russian troops under Alexander I. These still being worked on and they will be soon ready, distributed on twenty volumes approximately. Our new edition, the first ever published in English, both on paper and digital format, boasts a large number of color plates, many of them unpublished and coloured by our team of expert artists and scholars of uniformology. Each volume is based on 50/70 plates, always accompanied by the original translated text which describes the uniforms, the organization and the armament of the Russian army of the period.

A unique work in its genre, a must have in any respecting collection!

Aleksandr Vasilevich Viskovatov born 22 April (4 May New Style) 1804, died 27 February (11 March) 1858 in St. Petersburg, Russian military historian. He graduated from the 1st Cadet Corps and served in the artillery, the hydrographic depot of the Naval Ministry, and then in the Department of Military Educational Institutions.

He mainly studied historical artifacts and the histories of military units. Viskovatov's greatest work was the Historical Description of the Clothing and Arms of the Russian Army (Vols. 1-30, St. Petersburg, 1841-62; 2nd ed. Vols. 1-34, St. Petersburg - Novosibirsk - Leningrad, 1899-1948). This work is based on a great quantity of archival documents and contains four thousand colored illustrations.

Viskovatov was the author of Chronicles of the Russian Army (Books 1-20, St. Petersburg, 1834-42) and Chronicles of the Russian Imperial Army (Parts 1-7, St. Petersburg, 1852). He collected valuable material on the history of the Russian navy which went into A Short Overview of Russian Naval Campaigns and General Voyages to the End of the XVII Century (St. Petersburg, 1864; 2nd edition Moscow, 1946). Together with A.I. Mikhailovskii-Danilevskii he helped prepare and create the Military Gallery in the Winter Palace.

He wrote the historical military inscriptions for the walls of the Hall of St. George in the Great Palace of the Kremlin. (From the article in the Soviet Military Encyclopedia.)

CONTENTS

*

RUSSIAN ARMY, CAVALRY 1796-1801

Changes in the uniforms and equipment of Army Cavalry, Artillery, Engineers, and Garrisons, from 1796 to 1801

IV. Cuirassier regiments
V.   Dragoon regiments
VI. Hussar regiments

IV. CUIRASSIER REGIMENTS (Kirasirskie polki)

29 November 1796 – At the same time as a new set of Military Regulations (*Voinskii Ustav*) was promulgated, there were new directives regarding the clothing and weapons of Army Cuirassier Regiments. (Note: Here "Army" means "not Guards." – M.C.) These directives, with only the smallest changes, guided the formulation of the organizational authorization tables (*shtaty*) confirmed by HIGHEST authority on 5 January, and there were almost no changes for the rest of EMPEROR PAUL I's reign.

Based on the 1796 regulations and 1798 tables, a private **Cuirassier** was prescribed clothing, weapons, and accouterments as follows: *coat, waistcoat, breeches, boots, boot cuffs, gloves, hat with plume, cloak, forage cap, smock, warm coat, broad sword with sword knot, sword belt, sabertache, girdle, cuirass, carbine, cross belt, cartridge pouch with strap,* and in mounted order—a pair of *pistols. Horse furniture* and its appurtenances included: *saddle with saddle bucket, holsters, bridle, mouthpiece, cruppers, chestband, saddle girth, stirrups, cushion for the pack load,* and *horse cloth; shabrack, pistol holder covers, valise, forage sack, bag,* and *water flask.*

Coat (kolet) – at first prescribed to be of straw colored kersey (*palevaya kirza*) but from February 1797 of white kersey, and if there was a shortage of that material, then of white cloth. Cut exactly as already described for coats of Gatchina Cuirassiers or Gendarmes. It had a fold-down cloth collar sewn down on all four sides, slit cuffs, and two shoulder straps, all of the distinctive regimental color. Along the edges of the front opening from the neck to the waist, and along the edges of the *polki* or tails—wool galloon or tape (*galun ili bason*) 3/4 vershok (5/8 inch) wide (Illus. Nos. 1017 and 1018)(1).

Waistcoat (kamzol) – of the same pattern as for infantry except with small hooks instead of buttons. It was of cloth the same color as the collar and cuffs of the coat (2).

Breeches (shtany) – of deerskin (*losinnyi*) (3).

Boots (sapogi) – with blunt toes, bell tops, large heels, iron spurs, leather straps over and under the spurs (*nadshporniki i podshporniki*) (4).

Boot cuffs (shtibel'-manzhety) – of white shirt linen (5).

Neckcloth (galstuk) – of black cloth, unlined, tied with ribbon in the back (6).

Gloves (perchatki) – chamois, with gauntlet cuffs as for infantry non-commissioned officers except with pointed and not rounded ends or corners (7).

Hat (shlyapa) – three cornered, 4 vershoks (7 inches) high, with pointed corners bent downward; bound with a black woollen cord; tassels at the side corners, with their associated cord, of black and yellow wool (later—red wool); a cockade of black worsted ribbon with two orange edgings; with a button the same color as the facings on the officer's uniform; a plume of fine white cock feathers, with black and yellow feathers at the top or bottom (Illus. 1017 and 1019) (8).

Cloak (plashch) – of green cloth with a narrow standing collar the same color as the collar of the coat, and with a single flat brass button (Illus. 1020) (9).

Forage cap (furazhnaya shapka) – of the same pattern as for infantry, with a white top and a band the same color as the collar (Illus. 1021) (10).

Smock (kitel) – made from coarse calamanco (*kalamenko*), with a small standing collar and large flat covered buttons, six on each side of the front (Illus. 1021) (11).

Warm coat (fufaika) – for winter, of sheepskin (12).

Broadsword (palash) – of almost the same pattern as for Dragoons under EMPRESS CATHERINE II from 1778 to 1786, i.e. with a brass basket hilt ending at the top with an eagle's head; with a scabbard in steel mountings with rings for swordbelt straps (Illus. 1022) (13).

Sword knot (temlyak) – with a strap of black (later red) leather, and a tassel of twisted worsted: in the 1st or Leib-Squadron – white; 2nd – orange, 3rd – black, 4th – sky blue, and 5th – green (Illus. 1022) (14).

Swordbelt (portupeya) – of thick red Russian leather (*yuft'*) 1 vershok (1-3/4 inches) wide; fastened in front with a brass buckle and having on the left half three brass rings through which are passed five straps of the same red Russian leather, with brass buckles: two at the end for the broadsword and three in the middle for the sabertache (Illus. 1022) (15).

Sabertache (tashka) – of black leather with a covering of cloth the same color as the coat collar; trimmed with white woolen tape (*bason*) around the edges; with a crown, IMPERIAL monogram, and laurel wreath, all of yellow or white cloth (according to the color of the buttons), and with three brass rings at the top for the above mentioned straps (Illus. 1022). Width of the sabertache – 5 vershoks (8-3/4 inches), length in the middle - 6 vershoks (10-1/2 inches), length at the edges – 4-1/2 vershoks (7-7/8 inches) (16).

Girdle (kushak) – of stamin, the same color as the coat collar, 2 vershoks (3-1/2 inches) wide, 4 vershoks (7 inches) long, with pointed ends and three stripes along the whole length (Illus. 1022) (17).

Cuirass (kiras) – black, trimmed all around with red leather and lined with white quilted linen; held to the Cuirassier with the help of two deerskin straps. One strap was slit down almost its whole length into two halves and thus three ends were formed, of which the two narrow ones were fastened to the upper edges of the cuirass and the remaining wide one folded back in half to become a kind of loop. The other strap was passed through this loop and girded, so to speak, the Cuirassier, being fastened in front of the cuirass with a brass buckle and prong (Illus. 1022) (18).

Carbine (karabin) – with brass fittings, and with a *sling, lock cover (ognivnyi chekhol), and frizzen cover (polunagalishche)* all of red Russian leather. Length—1 arshin 14 vershoks (4 feet 3-3/8 inches) (Illus. 1022) (19).

Shoulder belt (pogonnaya perevyaz) – 2-1/2 vershoks (4 3/8 inches) wide, with brass buckle, frame, and end piece. Trimmed along the edges with wool tape (*bason*) 1/2 vershok (7/8 inch) wide, of the same color as the tape on the coat (Illus. 1022) (20).

Cartridge pouch (lyadunka) – for 30 cartridges, made from thick black leather; with the same brass plate on the cover as for infantry pouches except smaller. It had a deerskin strap 1-1/3 vershoks (2 1/3 inches) wide, with side stitching (*proshivki*) on the edges. As before, this strap was fastened to two brass rings sewn onto the sides of the pouch (Illus. 1022) (21).

Pistols (pistolety) – 12 3/4 vershoks (22 3/8 inches) long, with brass mountings and the EMPEROR'S monogram in the bend of the stock (*na izlozhine*) (Illus. 1022) (22).

Saddle (sedlo) – German, of the pattern for Russian Cuirassiers before the changes brought in by Prince Potemkin. It was of black leather; all straps and cushions black; iron bridle bits (*uzdechnyya udila*) and stirrups; curb bits likewise of iron, with brass disks (*bukli*) decorated with the image of a two-headed eagle; horse cloth (*popona*) of white cloth (23).

Shabrack (cheprak) and *pistol holder covers (chushki)* – of the pattern for infantry officers. Made from cloth, of the same color as the coat collar; trimmed around the edges with woolen tape and decorated with the same monogram and laurel wreath as on the sabertache, but without a crown (Illus. 1023) (24).

Valise (chemodan) – 1 arshin 2 vershoks (31-1/2 inches) long, 5 vershoks (8-3/4 inches) in diameter; of white cloth with four flat brass buttons (25).

Forage sack (furazhnyi sak) – of almost the same size as the valise, but made from coarse calamanco (26).

Bag (torba) for feeding the horse. Of thick linen (27).

Water flask (vodonosnaya flyazha) – wooden, wrapped or covered with leather (30).

In addition to the items listed here, each squadron was issued 16 tinned copper *kettles (mednye, luzhenye kotly)* with lids, 16 *sickles (kosy)* for gathering hay, and 20 *axes* (29).

Cuirassier horse (loshad' kirasirskaya) — prescribed to be of any color, at a price of 120 roubles (30).

Noncommissioned officers and first sergeants of Cuirassier regiments (unter-ofitsery i vakhmistry Kirasirskikh polkov) had the same uniform as cuirassier privates, but without shoulder straps and with gold or silver galloon on the collar and cuffs of the coat, according to the distinctions on the officers' uniforms. Tassels on the hat were white with a center of black and orange worsted (*garus*). They also had the additional distinction of the black and orange feathers being at the top of the plume instead of at the bottom (Illus. 1023). Like infantry non-commissioned officers, they were authorized a cane (*trost'*) which in mounted order was fastened by a wrist strap to the butt of the right-hand pistol, with the lower end passed through one or another strap, most probably the horse's chest band (*paperst'*). Of the weapons and accouterments of private cuirassiers, they did not have the carbine, crossbelt, and cartridge pouch, but instead they had, under each holster beneath the pistol carriers, six places for cartridges. Also, their saddles had no saddle buckets (31).

Distinguished officer candidates (estandart-yunkera) were uniformed and armed, and had the same horse furniture, as noncommissioned officers, except that the coat had a shoulder strap on the left, and the saddle had a bucket (*bushmat*) for a standard (*shtandart*). To this last item belonged a 3-arshin (84-inch) wide deerskin crossbelt or *bandoleer (pantaler)* with brass buckle, frame, and end piece, with an iron hook, and with galloon on the edges, gold or silver according to the color of the fringe on the standard (Illus. 1024) (32).

Trumpeters trubachi) were uniformed as private cuirassiers, but their coats had two false sleeves (*lopasti*) in the back and tape (*bason*) along all edges and seams, as well as on the sleeves and at the shoulder. The same tape was around the waistcoat. Regardless of the plume itself, there was red plumage around the hat's edge (Illus. 1024). Of cuirassier weapons and accouterments, they were prescribed only the broadsword, sword belt, and sabertache. Their saddles had no buckets, while *trumpets* (*truby*) had worsted tassels and cords in two colors: white and the collar of the coat's collar and cuffs (33).

Staff trumpeter (*shtabnyi trubach* or *shtab-trubach*) – distinguished from squadron trumpeters only in that, like non-commissioned officers, they had gold or silver galloon on the coat's collar and cuffs. The plume had a top part of black and yellow feathers; non-commissioned officer's tassels on the hat, and a cane (Illus. 1025) (34).

Kettledrummer (*litavrshchik*) – all the same uniform clothing, weapons, and accouterments as squadron trumpeters, but the coat was without false sleeves and the saddle without holsters. Kettledrums (*litavry*) remained as before, i.e. of red copper and weighing 1 pood 10 funty (46 pounds), while their *drum banners* (*zanavesy*) were made of material the same color as the coat collar, with gold or silver monograms, galloon, and fringes according to the appointments on officers' uniforms (Illus. 1026) (35).

Officers wore a *coat* (*kolet*) of straw-colored (*palevyi*) cloth, later white, with collar and cuffs the same color as prescribed for lower ranks, velvet *lining* to the small tails, and gold or silver galloon down the front opening. Cloth *waistcoat* the same color as the collar, trimmed on the edges with galloon; deerskin *breeches*; *boots* with bell tops and silver or silvered spurs; *gaiter tops* (*shtibel'-manzhety*); chamois *gloves* with gauntlet cuffs; black *neck cloth* of serge (*sarzhevyi*). The *hat* had a ribbon or cockade, and a button loop and button, similar to those for generals in the infantry, with tassels of *solot* (unknown meaning – M.C.) and black silk, later of silver and black silk, with orange. The same plumes as private cuirassiers (Illus. 1027 and 1028). Along with this were prescribed: *broadsword*, with a gilt hilt decorated with the image of a two-headed eagle, and with brass or steel mountings to the scabbard, in accordance with the uniform's appointments (Illus. 1029); *sword knot*, similar to that for an infantry officer but with a flat tassel instead of rounded, and instead of a strap of silver lace—one of black leather, with silver sewn down both edges; deerskin *sword belt* and black *cuirass* (*kiras*) with red cloth lining or trim, along which, in manner similar to galloon, were brass fittings affixed with brass nails of pointed or conical form (Illus. 1029). Similar nails were used to affix a brass plate to deerskin straps that served to fasten the cuirass, and in the front of the cuirass, in an oval surrounded by an armature of military trophies, was the image of a two-headed eagle (Illus. 1029) (36). The *sash* (*sharf*) was the same as for infantry officers, and the *saddle* and all horse furniture straps were black. The bit and stirrups were iron; disks on the mouthpiece were gilded. Shabracks (*cepraki*) and pistol holders (*chushki*) were of cloth the same color as prescribed for lower ranks, with gold or silver galloon and monograms to match the galloon on the coat (37). Apart from the *full combatant* (*polnaya stroevaya*) uniform described here, cuirassier officers also had an *everyday* (*vsednevnaya*) one used when not on duty. This uniform consisted of a white cloth double-breasted *undress coat* (*vitse-mundir*) or caftan (*kaftan*) with a fall-down collar, lapels, and slit cuffs the same color as the *kolet* coat collar. It had an aiguillette and buttons the same color as the galloon on the coat, with turned back skirts lined with stamin that with yellow buttons was the same color as the collar but with white buttons was straw-colored (Illus. 1030). With this undress coat was worn a straw-colored cloth *waistcoat* with flat buttons, white cloth breeches, an *epee* (*shpaga*) like that for infantry except with cups that become narrow toward the front. A *cane* and—already described above—*hat, neck cloth, gloves*, and *boots* (38).

Like the lower ranks, all officers powdered their **hair** and gathered it into *curls* and a *queue* (*pukly i kosa*) braided with black silk ribbon. *Generals*, as in the infantry, were distinguished only by white plumage (*plyumazh*) on the hat (Illus. 1030) (39).

Non-combatant ranks (*nestroevye chiny*), namely squadron *medics* (*fel'dshera*) and the regimental *saddler* (*sedel'nik*), *armorer* (*ruzheinyi master*), and *provost* (*profos*), as well as *wagon drivers* (*pogonshchiki*) or *train personnel* (*furleity*), were uniformed in the manner of non-combatants in infantry regiments, except that they had cuirassier pattern hats (40).

Of *non-combatant officer ranks*, the *regimental Quartermaster* (*polkovyi Kvartermeister*) and *Auditor* (*Auditor*) were uniformed as Quartermasters and Auditors, and the *Doctor* (*Lekar'*) as for Doctors, in Army infantry, except that they had the different hat prescribed for cavalry. The *stablemaster* (*shtalmeister*) was prescribed the same coat as the Doctor but with dark-green worsted buttons (Illus. 1031) (41).

Along with these regulations for the uniforms and weapons of Cuirassier regiments, they were the following **distinctions** between them:

In HIS MAJESTY'S Leib-Cuirassier Regiment: For lower ranks—sky-blue (*goluboi*) collar, cuffs, shoulder straps, waistcoat, sash, sabertache, shabrack, and pistol holders; white lace (*bason*) with sky-blue stripes and checks (Illus. 1017). *For officers*—collar, cuffs, and skirt turnback lining of sky-blue velvet; silver appointments; gallon with indentations on shabracks and pistol holders (Illus. 1017) (42).

In HER MAJESTY'S Leib-Cuirassier Regiment: For lower ranks—raspberry (*malinovyi*) collar, cuffs, shoulder straps, waistcoat, sash, sabertache, shabrack, and pistol holders; white lace with raspberry stripes and checks (Illus. 1019). *For officers*—collar, cuffs, and skirt turnback lining of raspberry velvet; silver appointments; gallon with indentations on shabracks and pistol holders (Illus. 1020) (43).

In the Military Order Cuirassier Regiment: For lower ranks—black collar, cuffs, shoulder straps, waistcoat, sash, sabertache, shabrack, and pistol holders; coat lace with two black stripes and one white; on the sabertache—yellow, and on the shabrack and pistol holders—yellow with a black stripe (Illus. 1023). *For officers*—collar, cuffs, and skirt turnback lining of black velvet; gold appointments (Illus. 1023); gallon with indentations on shabracks and pistol holders (44).

In the Yekaterinoslav Regiment: For lower ranks—orange collar, cuffs, shoulder straps, waistcoat, sash, sabertache, shabrack, and pistol holders; coat lace with two orange stripes and one white; on the sabertache—white, and on the shabrack and pistol holders—white with an orange stripe (Illus. 1024). *For officers*—collar, cuffs, and skirt turnback lining of orange velvet; silver appointments; gallon with indentations on shabracks and pistol holders (45).

In the Kazan Regiment: For lower ranks—raspberry collar, cuffs, shoulder straps, waistcoat, sash, sabertache, shabrack, and pistol holders; coat lace raspberry; on the sabertache—yellow, and on the shabrack and pistol holders—yellow with a raspberry stripe (Illus. 1024). *For officers*—collar, cuffs, and skirt turnback lining of raspberry velvet; gold appointments; gallon without indentations on shabracks and pistol holders (46).

In the Ryazan Regiment: For lower ranks—sky-blue collar, cuffs, shoulder straps, waistcoat, sash, sabertache, shabrack, and pistol holders; coat lace with two sky-blue stripes and one white; on the sabertache—yellow, and on the shabrack and pistol holders—yellow with a sky-blue stripe (Illus. 1025). *For officers*—collar, cuffs, and skirt turnback lining of sky-blue velvet; gold appointments; gallon without indentations on shabracks and pistol holders (47).

In the Yamburg Regiment: For lower ranks—herring-grey (*seladonovyi*) collar, cuffs, shoulder straps, waistcoat, sash, sabertache, shabrack, and pistol holders; coat lace herring grey; on the sabertache—yellow, and on the shabrack and pistol holders—yellow with a herring-grey stripe. *For officers*—collar, cuffs, and skirt turnback lining of herring-grey velvet; gold appointments; gallon without indentations on shabracks and pistol holders (48).

In the Glukhov Regiment: For lower ranks—herring-grey collar, cuffs, shoulder straps, waistcoat, sash, sabertache, shabrack, and pistol holders; coat lace of two herring-grey stripes and one white; on the sabertache—white, and on the shabrack and pistol holders—white with a herring-grey stripe (Illus. 1025). *For officers*—collar, cuffs, and skirt turnback lining of herring-grey velvet; silver appointments; gallon without indentations on shabracks and pistol holders (49).

In the Kiev Regiment: For lower ranks—Yellow collar, cuffs, shoulder straps, waistcoat, sash, sabertache, shabrack, and pistol holders; coat lace yellow; on the sabertache—white, and on the shabrack and pistol holders—white with a yellow stripe (Illus. 1026). *For officers*—collar, cuffs, and skirt turnback lining of yellow velvet; silver appointments; gallon without indentations on shabracks and pistol holders (50).

In the Nezhin Regiment: For lower ranks—Violet (*fioletovyi*) collar, cuffs, shoulder straps, waistcoat, sash, sabertache, shabrack, and pistol holders; coat lace with two violet stripes and one white; on the sabertache—yellow, and on the shabrack and pistol holders—yellow with a violet stripe (Illus. 1026). *For officers*—collar, cuffs, and skirt turnback lining of violet velvet; gold appointments; gallon without indentations on shabracks and pistol holders (51).

In the Sofiya Regiment: For lower ranks—Orange collar, cuffs, shoulder straps, waistcoat, sash, sabertache, shabrack, and pistol holders; coat lace with two orange stripes and one white; on the sabertache—yellow, and on the shabrack and pistol holders—yellow with an orange stripe. *For officers*—collar, cuffs, and skirt turnback lining of orange velvet; gold appointments; gallon without indentations on shabracks and pistol holders (Illus. 1027) (52).

In the Starodub Regiment: For lower ranks—red collar, cuffs, shoulder straps, waistcoat, sash, sabertache, shabrack, and pistol holders; coat lace red; on the sabertache—white, and on the shabrack and pistol holders—white with a red stripe. *For officers*—collar, cuffs, and skirt turnback lining of red velvet; silver appointments (Illus. 1027); gallon without indentations on shabracks and pistol holders (Illus. 1027) (53).

In the Chernigov Regiment: For lower ranks—Violet collar, cuffs, shoulder straps, waistcoat, sash, sabertache, shabrack, and pistol holders; coat lace violet; on the sabertache—white, and on the shabrack and pistol holders—white with a violet stripe. *For officers*—collar, cuffs, and skirt turnback lining of violet velvet; silver appointments (Illus. 1028); gallon without indentations on shabracks and pistol holders (54).

In the Riga Regiment: For lower ranks—Red collar, cuffs, shoulder straps, waistcoat, sash, sabertache, shabrack, and pistol holders; coat lace with two red stripes and one white; on the sabertache— yellow, and on the shabrack and pistol holders—yellow with a red stripe. *For officers*—collar, cuffs, and skirt turnback lining of red velvet; gold appointments (Illus. 1028); gallon without indentations on shabracks and pistol holders (55).

In the Kharkov Regiment: For lower ranks—Black collar, cuffs, shoulder straps, waistcoat, sash, sabertache, shabrack, and pistol holders; coat lace black; on the sabertache—white, and on the shabrack and pistol holders—white with a black stripe. *For officers*—collar, cuffs, and skirt turnback lining of black velvet; silver appointments (Illus. 1030); gallon without indentations on shabracks and pistol holders (56).

In the Little-Russia Regiment: For lower ranks—Yellow collar, cuffs, shoulder straps, waistcoat, sash, sabertache, shabrack, and pistol holders; coat lace with two yellow stripes and one white; on the sabertache, shabrack, and pistol holders—yellow. *For officers*—collar, cuffs, and skirt turnback lining of yellow velvet; gold appointments (Illus. 1030); gallon without indentations on shabracks and pistol holders (57).

5 January 1798 – With the introduction of the *Regimental Wagon Master (Polkovyi Vagenmeister)* into the organizational table for Cuirassier regiments, he was prescribed the same uniform and weapons as non-commissioned officers. Along with this, for all ranks the green cloaks were replaced by white ones (58).

In the **three Cuirassier regiments** (Lieutenant General Neplyuev's, Major General Friderici's, and Major General Zorn's) established on **20 August 1798**, the colors for uniforms were as follows:

In Neplyuev's Regiment: For lower ranks—Dark-blue (*sinii*) collar, cuffs, shoulder straps, waistcoat, sash, sabertache, shabrack, and pistol holders; coat lace dark blue; on the sabertache—white, and on the shabrack and pistol holders— white with a dark-blue stripe (Illus. 1032). *For officers*— collar, cuffs, and skirt turnback lining of dark-blue velvet; silver appointments; gallon without indentations on shabracks and pistol holders (59).

In Friderici's Regiment: For lower ranks—Dark-blue (*sinii*) collar, cuffs, shoulder straps, waistcoat, sash, sabertache, shabrack, and pistol holders; coat lace with two dark-blue stripes and one white (Illus. 1032); on the sabertache—yellow, and on the shabrack and pistol holders— yellow with a dark-blue stripe. *For officers*—collar, cuffs, and skirt turnback lining of dark-blue velvet; gold appointments; gallon without indentations on shabracks and pistol holders (60).

In Zorn's Regiment: For lower ranks—Dark-green collar, cuffs, shoulder straps, waistcoat, sash, sabertache, shabrack, and pistol holders; coat lace with two dark-green stripes and one white (Illus. 1032); on the sabertache—yellow, and on the shabrack and pistol holders— yellow with a dark-green stripe. *For officers*—collar, cuffs, and skirt turnback lining of green velvet; gold appointments; gallon without indentations on shabracks and pistol holders (61).

8 October 1798 – As a sign of HIGHEST benevolence, **HER MAJESTY'S Leib-Cuirassier Regiment** was granted, in place of the monograms on sabertaches, pistol holders, and shabracks, eight-pointed *stars* with a black two-headed eagle in the center on an orange field. For lower ranks the stars were white, and for officers—silver (Illus. 1033) (62).

9 October 1799 – The "acorns" (*shishki*) above the tassels on officers' **sashes, sword knots** and **hat tassels**, and on the **sword knots** of lower ranks, were ordered to be raspberry, and there were to be three colors in the stripes and tassels: black, orange, and raspberry (64).

11 February 1801 – **HIS MAJESTY'S Leib-Cuirassier Regiment** was ordered to have, on sabertaches, shabracks, and pistol holders, *stars* of the pattern granted to HER MAJESTY'S Leib-Cuirassier Regiment (65).

V. DRAGOON REGIMENTS (Dragunskie polki)

At the same time as for Cuirassiers, there were changes in the uniforms and weapons of *Dragoon regiments*. Based on these changes, each private *dragoon* was prescribed: *coat* of the color and pattern for jägers, with an aiguillette the same color as the buttons, with a shoulder strap—and for lower ranks also lapels—of the same color as the collar and cuffs, and with straw-colored kersey lining (Illus. 1034); *waistcoat*, of the pattern for infantry, of straw-colored cloth; deerskin *breeches*, and in case of a shortage of deerskin—goatskin or other buckskin-like leather; *boots, gaiter tops, neck cloth, gloves, hat, forage cap, smock, warm coat*, and *cloak*—all of the patterns for cuirassiers except for the last item being all green, and the gloves the same color as the waistcoat (66).

Weapons and *accouterments* consisted of: *broadsword*, similar to that for cuirassiers but with a lion's head on the hilt instead of an eagle's, and with a scabbard that instead of iron fittings had only a brass hook and endpiece inserted under the leather; *sword knot* in an infantry *sword belt* with a bayonet scabbard, finished with ochre the same color as the waistcoat; *musket (mushket)* 2 arshins (56 inches) long without the bayonet and 2-1/2 arshins (70 inches) with the bayonet, with brass mountings, iron bar (*zheleznyi pogon*), and sling (Illus. 1035), firelock cover and frizzen cover of Russian leather; *cartridge pouch* of thick black leather of the same size and appearance as for cuirassiers, and a *cartridge-pouch belt* the same color as the waistcoat, of the same width as cuirassier cross belt, and with the same buckle, frame, endpiece, and hook. *Pistols, saddle*, and all other horse furniture were the same as those prescribed for Cuirassier regiments except that the first item was a little smaller, while the *shabrack* and *pistol covers* had no monograms and instead of tape—cloth trim around the edges (Illus. 1034) (67). A *dragoon horse* was prescribed to cost from 60 to 80 roubles (68). *Non-commssioned officers, the supply sergeant (fur'er)*, and *sergeant (vakhtmeister)*, while wearing the same uniform as private dragoons, were distinguished by gold or silver (according to the color of the buttons) galloon along the edges of the collar, cuffs, and pocket flaps, and furthermore—by the black and yellow feathers on their plumes being at the top rather than at the base (Illus. 1036) (69). Of dragoon weapons and accouterments, they were not authorized the carbine and pouch, in place of which they had, on the holsters, six places for pistol cartridges. Also, their sword belts had no frog for a bayonet scabbard nor did their saddles have a saddle bucket (*bushmat*). Like cuirassier non-commissioned officers, they were prescribed to have canes (70).

Distinguished officer candidate (fanen-yunker)—the same uniform, weapons, and horse furniture as for the preceding non-commissioned officers but the saddle had a bucket for a standard, and they had a deerskin cross belt for the latter item similar to that for cuirassiers but without trim (Illus. 1037) (71).

Drummers (barabanshchiki) were uniformed as private dragoons but with wings (*kryl'tsy*) on the shoulders the same color as the collar, a strap on the right shoulder, and four sewn-on stripes (*nashivki*) on each sleeve, of white woolen tape (*bason*) with stripes with a zigzag line (*zmeika*) between them, also the same color as the collar. The exact same tape was sewn onto the wings (Illus. 1038). Weapons, accouterments, and horse furniture—the same as for non-commissioned officers, with the *drum, cross belt*, and *apron* the same as for infantry drummers, the first with tooth-shaped triangles on the hoops in two colors: light green and the color of the collar (72).

Trumpeters (trubachi) had the uniform, weapons, and horse furniture all similar to those for drummers except for red plumage around the hat and no shoulder strap or wings on the coat. There were two false sleeves on the back of the coat, which was trimmed with tape: along all seams; the edges of the collar, cuffs, and pocket flaps; on the false sleeves; and on the breast around the button holes, with these last having small tassels the same color as the tape (Illus. 1039). *Trumpets (truby)* were the same as in Cuirassier regiments, with worsted cords colored white and the two regimental colors, i.e. light green and that prescribed for the collar (73).

Staff-trumpeter (stab-trubach)—everything the same as for squadron trumpeters except that the coat had gold or silver galloon (according to the color of the buttons) on the collar, cuffs, and pocket flaps. The top of the plume was of black and yellow feathers, and a cane was authorized (Illus. 1040) (74).

Hautboy players (goboisty) had the same as for trumpeters except that the coat had no false sleeves and the hat no plumage (Illus. 1041) (75).

Kettledrummer (litavrshchik)—uniformed and armed as the trumpeters, but his coat had no false sleeves (Illus. 1042). The horse furniture and kettledrums were of the patterns prescribed for kettledrummers in Cuirassier regiments, i.e. the saddle had no holsters. The drum banners *(zanavesy)* were the same color as the collar, with embroidery, galloon, and fringes the color of the buttons (76).

Officers had the same coat as private dragoons but without a shoulder strap, and with gilt or silvered buttons and an aiguillette in the same color. Straw-colored *waistcoat*, with the same color buttons as on the coat. Deerskin *breeches*, whitened. *Boots, gaiter tops, neck cloth, sword knot,* and *sash*—the exact same patterns as for officers in Cuirassier regiments, while *gloves, sword belt,* and *broadsword* were similar to those for dragoons except that the last item had a gilt hilt, hook, and end piece. *Horse furniture* was prescribed to be the same as for Cuirassier officers. In all regiments *shabracks* and *pistol holders* had flat galloon (the same color as the buttons), without toothed indentations and with sewn-on silver tracery, with a gold or silver (according to the galloon) cord instead of monograms (Illus. 1043 and 1044) (77).

Generals were distinguished from officers only by white plumage around the hat (Illus. 1045) (78). All **combatant** ranks in Dragoon regiments wore their coats, with officers adding a sash, according to the time of year, in the exact same manner as in the infantry (79).

Uniforms for **non-combatant** lower ranks (*regimental saddler, armorer, spur maker (shpornyi master), provost, squadron medics,* and *wagon drivers* or *train personnel*) as well as for non-combatants in officer ranks (regimental *Quartermaster, Auditor,* and *Doctor*) were exactly the same as for these ranks in Cuirassier regiments (80).

Colors and other **distinctions** prescribed for Dragoon regiments were as follows:

In the Vladimir Regiment:

For lower ranks—coat with sky-blue collar, lapels, cuffs, and shoulder strap; yellow aiguillette and buttons; sky-blue shabrack and pistol holders, with white trim (Illus. 1034). *For officers*—gold buttonhole loops, with small tassels (Illus. 1034) (81).

In the Astrakhan Regiment:

For lower ranks—coat with yellow collar, lapels, cuffs, and shoulder strap; white aiguillette and buttons; yellow shabrack and pistol holders, with white trim (Illus. 1036). *For officers*—silver buttonhole loops, with small tassels (Illus. 1036) (82).

In the Nizhnii-Novgorod Regiment:
For lower ranks—coat with black collar, cuffs, and shoulder strap, no lapels; white aiguillette and buttons; black shabrack and pistol holders, with white trim (Illus. 1037). *For officers*—silver buttonhole loops, with small tassels (Illus. 1036) (83).

In the Pskov Regiment:
For lower ranks—coat with red cloth collar, cuffs, and shoulder strap, no lapels; yellow aiguillette and buttons (Illus. 1038); red shabrack and pistol holders, with yellow trim. *For officers*—gold buttonhole loops with small tassels, and worsted velvet (*tripovyi*) collar and cuffs (84).

In the St.-Peterburg Regiment:
For lower ranks—coat with rose pink (*rozovyi*) collar, cuffs, and shoulder strap, no lapels; yellow aiguillette and buttons; rose pink shabrack and pistol holders, with yellow trim. *For officers*—gold buttonhole loops, with small tassels (Illus. 1039) (85).

In the Smolensk Regiment:
For lower ranks—coat with orange (*oranzhevyi*) collar, lapels, cuffs, and shoulder strap; yellow aiguillette and buttons (Illus. 1039); orange shabrack and pistol holders, with yellow trim. *For officers*—gold buttonhole loops, with small tassels (86).

In the Taganrog Regiment:
For lower ranks—coat with yellow collar, lapels, cuffs, and shoulder strap; yellow aiguillette and buttons; yellow shabrack and pistol holders, with likewise yellow trim. *For officers*—gold buttonhole loops, with small tassels (87).

In the Irkutsk Regiment:
For lower ranks—coat with white collar, cuffs, and shoulder strap, no lapels; yellow aiguillette and buttons (Illus. 1041); white shabrack and pistol holders, with yellow trim. *For officers*—gold buttonhole loops, without small tassels (Illus. 1041) (88).

In the Orenburg Regiment:
For lower ranks—coat with black collar, lapels, cuffs, and shoulder strap; yellow aiguillette and buttons (Illus. 1042); black shabrack and pistol holders, with yellow trim. *For officers*—gold buttonhole loops, with small tassels (89).

In the Siberia Regiment:
For lower ranks—coat with white collar, cuffs, and shoulder strap, no lapels; white aiguillette and buttons (Illus. 1042); white shabrack and pistol holders, with likewise white trim. *For officers*—silver buttonhole loops, with small tassels (90).

In the Ingermanland Regiment:
For lower ranks—coat with raspberry (*malinovyi*) collar, lapels, cuffs, and shoulder strap; white aiguillette and buttons (Illus. 1042); raspberry shabrack and pistol holders, with white trim. *For officers*—silver buttonhole loops, with small tassels (91).

In the Narva Regiment:
For lower ranks—coat with sky-blue collar, lapels, cuffs, and shoulder strap; white aiguillette and buttons; sky-blue shabrack and pistol holders, with white trim. *For officers*—silver buttonhole loops, without small tassels (Illus. 1043) (92).

In the Rostov Regiment:
For lower ranks—coat with red cloth collar, lapels, cuffs, and shoulder strap; white aiguillette and

buttons; red cloth shabrack and pistol holders, with white trim. *For officers*—silver buttonhole loops with small tassels, and worsted velvet lapels and cuffs (Illus. 1043) (93).

In the Moscow Regiment:

For lower ranks—coat with rose pink collar, cuffs, and shoulder strap, no lapels; white aiguillette and buttons; rose pink shabrack and pistol holders, with white trim. *For officers*—silver buttonhole loops, with small tassels (Illus. 1044) (94).

In the Seversk Regiment:

For lower ranks—coat with orange collar, lapels, cuffs, and shoulder strap; white aiguillette and buttons; orange shabrack and pistol holders, with white trim. *For officers*—silver buttonhole loops, with small tassels (Illus. 1045) (95).

In the Kargopol Regiment:

For lower ranks—coat with raspberry collar, lapels, cuffs, and shoulder strap; white aiguillette and buttons; raspberry shabrack and pistol holders, with white trim. *For officers*—silver buttonhole loops, with small tassels (Illus. 1045) (96).

5 January 1798 – The *Wagon Masters (Vagenmeistery)* introduced into the organizational table for Dragoon regiments were prescribed the same uniforms, accouterments, and weapons as combatant non-commissioned officers. The green cloaks were replaced by white ones and the price of a horse for combatant dragoons was set at 60 roubles (97).

29 May 1798 – In the *Nizhnii-Novgorod Dragoon* Regiment, the black color of collars, cuffs, shoulder straps, shabracks, and pistol holders was changed to orange (98).

In the **two Dragoon regiments** (Major General Schreiders' and Major General Khastatov's) established on **20 August 1798**, the colors for uniforms were as follows:

In Schreiders' Regiment:

For lower ranks—coat with rose pink collar, lapels, cuffs and shoulder straps; yellow aiguillette and buttons (Illus. 1046); rose pink shabrack, and pistol holders, with yellow trim. *For officers*— gold buttonhole loops, with small tassels (99).

In Khastatov's Regiment: For lower ranks—coat with rose pink collar, lapels, cuffs and shoulder straps; white aiguillette and buttons (Illus. 1046); rose pink shabrack, and pistol holders, with white trim. *For officers*— silver buttonhole loops, with small tassels (100).

31 January 1799 – The cloaks established by the warrant of 5 January 1798 were replaced by dark-green *greatcoats* of the same pattern as for cuirassiers (101).

9 October 1799 - The acorn **knots** (*shishki*) on officers' sashes and on lower ranks' **sword knots**,were ordered to be raspberry-colored, and stripes and tassels were to be in three colors: black, orange, and raspberry (102).

3 April 1800 – The **ten-squadron Dragoon regiments** formed by joining two five-squadron regiments were ordered to have uniforms as follows:

Obrezkov's Regiment, formed from the former Vladimir and Taganrog regiments—the uniform of the Vladimir regiment (Illus. 1034) (103).

Pushkin's Regiment, formed from the former Narva and Nizhnii-Novgorod regiments—the uniform of the Nizhnii-Novgorod regiment (Illus. 1037 and the entry for 29 May 1798) (104).

Sacken 2nd's Regiment, formed from the former Irkutsk and Siberia regiments—the uniform of the Siberia rregiment (Illus. 1042) (105).

VI. HUSSAR REGIMENTS (Gusarskie polki)

At the beginning of EMPEROR PAUL I's reign all **Army Hussar regiments** received uniforms of almost exactly the same pattern and style as those of the Gatchina hussars. Uniform items, arms, and accouterments prescribed for a private *hussar* comprised: *pelisse, dolman, chakchiry breeches, boots, neck cloth, headdress, forage cap, cloak, warm coat, saber, sword knot, sword belt, sabertache, barrel sash, carbine, cross belt, cartridge pouch,* and a pair of pistols; *horse furniture* consisted of: *saddle, with holsters* and other appurtenances; *saddle cloth, valise, forage sack, feed bag,* and *water flask.*

The *pelisse (mentiya)* was made of cloth of a different color for each regiment, with a standing collar and sheepskin trim (white in almost all the regiments); worsted cords with fifteen large round buttons and thirty small flat buttons, yellow or tinned (Illus. 1047) (106).

Dolman (dulaman)—of cloth, also of a different color for each regiment, with standing collar and pointed cuffs; worsted cords with 45 buttons a little smaller than those on the pelisse; trimmed with red leather at the elbows and around the hooks and eyes (Illlus. 1047) (107).

Breeches (chakchiry)—of white cloth (Illus. 1047) (108).

Boots (sapogi)—with blunt toes, knee length, with a notch cut out at the back, and with iron spurs driven in (Illus. 1047) (109).

Neck cloth (galstuk)—of black cloth, no trim, tied with ribbons at the back (110).

Headdress (shapka)—5-1/2 vershoks (9-5/8 inches) high, trimmed with black dog hair (*sobachii mekh*); a cloth top or *bag (meshok)* the same color as the dolman; with two worsted cords and tassels the same color as the cords on the dolman; and with a plume of fine white feathers (Illus. 1047 and 1048) (111).

Forage cap (shapka furazhnaya)—of cloth, the same pattern as for infantry, and the same color as the pelisse; with or without a band (112).

Cloak (plashch)—of white cloth, of the pattern for cuirassiers and dragoons (113).

Warm coat (fufaika)—for winter, of sheepskin (114).

Saber (sablya)—1 arshin 4 vershoks (35 inches) long (from the base of the hilt to the tip of the blade); with a steel hilt and iron mountings on the scabbard (Illus. 1049) (115).

Sword knot (temlyak)—of red Russian leather, with a similar tassel (116).

Sword belt (portupeya)—also of red Russian leather; 3/4 vershok (1-3/8 inches) wide, with a brass hook for fastening, and with three brass rings for fitting the straps: two holding the saber and three the sabertache (117).

Sabertache—of plain unblackened leather with cloth over the cover in the same color as the dolman, with cloth trim that is flat in some regiments but toothed in others; and with an IMPERIAL monogram and crown the same color as the trim (Illus. 1049 and 1054) (118).

Barrel sash, or girdle (poyas)—of thin worsted cords with cross ties or bindings, or with slides (*s perevyazkami ili perevivkami, inache gombami*); with two cords and tassels the same color as the latter parts, and with two toggles for fastening (Illus. 1049) (119).

Carbine (karabin)—with brass fittings, iron ramrod, and a likewise iron bar with ring (Illus. 1049); and with a frizzen cover of black leather from a cow that has not yet calved (120).

Shoulder belt (pogonnaya perevyaz')—deerskin, of the pattern for cuirassiers except narrower and without trim; with a brass buckle, frame, and end piece, and an iron hook (121).

Cartridge pouch (lyadunka)—of red Russian leather and a similar strap passed through two brass rings fastened to the sides; with places for twenty cartridges, and with a small iron rammer or ramrod (*priboinik ili shampol*) for pistols (Illus. 1049) (122).

Pistols (pistolety)—10-1/2 vershoks (18-3/8 inches) long, with brass fittings and without a ramrod (Illus. 1049) (123).

Saddle (sedlo)—without a saddle bucket; of black leather, as are the holsters and all straps; with iron buckles and stirrups (124).

Saddle cloth (valtrap)—of cloth, usually the same color as the pelisse; with toothed cloth *trim* in a regimental color; with *piping* around the teeth of the very same cord as prescribed for dolmans, and with IMPERIAL crowns and monograms in the corners or wings, the same color as the cord (Illus. 1049 and 1054) (125).

Valise (chemodan)—of white cloth, with four buttons covered with the same (126).

Forage sack and *feed bag (furazhnyi sak i torba)*—canvas (127).

Water flask (vodonosnaya flyazha)—of wood and lined with black leather; with a likewise black leather strap and an iron buckle (128).

Hussar horse (loshad' gusarskaya)—authorized to be of any color at a price from 30 to 50 roubles (129).

Non-commissioned officers, the quartermaster, distinguished officer candidate, and *sergeant (Unter-ofitsery, kvartermistr, shandart-yunker i vakhmistr)* were distinguished from private hussars by gold or silver galloon (according to the color of the buttons) on pelisses and dolmans: along the lower half of the collar and on the sleeves—1/2 vershok (7/8 inch) wide, and on the breast behind the buttons—narrow, the same width as the cord (Illus. 1050). All these ranks wore chamois gloves with gauntlet cuffs and carried a cane, but did not have a carbine, cross strap, or cartridge pouch, in place of which there were places for six pistol cartridges on each of the holsters under the saddle cloth (130).

Squadron trumpeters (eskadronnye trubachi)—prescribed everything as for non-commissioned officer ranks, and distinguished from non-commissioned officers only by wings or shells (*rakoviny*) on the pelisse's shoulders, of worsted galloon the same color as the cords; they did not have gloves or canes. –Their *trumpets (truby)* were brass with cords and tassels the same color of the cords on the dolman (Illus. 1051) (131).

Staff-trumpeter (shtab-trubach)—also of non-commissioned officer rank, he had all the same uniform clothing, weapons, accouterments, and horse furniture as squadron trumpeters but with the addition of gloves and a cane, and with the exception of the trumpeter, which he was not authorized (Illus. 1052) (132).

None of the ranks named here powdered their hair. By previous long-time hussar custom, they wore their hair in long twisted temple locks (*viski*) and short queues (*kosy*) tied with a black ribbon about level with the neck cloth (Illus. 1048) (133).

Officers (ofitsery)—uniforms of the exact same colors and cut as for private hussars but all cords, tassels, and buttons were gold or silver, according to the color of the lower ranks' buttons. On the pelisse and dolman there was galloon and a fine fringe along the sides of the chest. The trim on the pelisse was of fox fur, and on the headdress—sable. In the base of the plume were black and orange feathers. The barrel sash was of silver cords with black and orange silk, and silver slides. The saber had a gilt hilt and brass or steel mountings on the scabbard, according to the color of the buttons. The sword knot was of the pattern for infantry officers. The sword belt, sabertache, and their suspension slings were of red morocco leather (*saf'yan*). On sabertaches and saddle cloths, instead of monograms, were sewn two-headed eagles with crowns—the former of gold, silver, and black silk, and the latter of only gold (Illus. 1053 and 1054). In parade order they used black leather *sarsamy* (decorative harness) as part of their horse furniture (134).

When not in formation, officers of Hussar regiments had the right to wear cloth *vengerki* coats lined with red stamin. These *vengerki* coats were of the color prescribed for the pelisse and had this item's buttons, cords, and galloon, with the addition of fur lining in the winter. In the back, they were completely closed without a rear opening, while in the front they had skirts folded upwards to that both knees could be seen; with the ends fastened by buttons. When wearing these coats, officers were without sashes and sabertaches, and wore the normal cavalry hats described above (Illus. 1055) (135).

Generals were distinguished from officers only by the hat having a high plume of straight white ostrich feathers with small black and yellow cock feathers at the base, stuck into a metal tube, or *chelenga*, with two-headed black eagle and a gold eagle's wing, similar to those for Leib-Hussars of the time of EMPRESS CATHERINE II (Illus. 1056 and 1057) (136).

Officers and generals of Hussar regiments both *powdered* their hair and wore the same *curls* and *queues* as in the heavy cavalry, except that the latter were shorter (137).

Uniform clothing for the **non-combatant** lower ranks: *armorer, squadron medics, and farriers* (*ruzheinyi master i eskadronnye fel'dshera i konovaly*), of which the last were of non-commissioned officer rank—as well as of those non-combatants holding officer rank: *Regimental Quartermaster, Auditor,* and *Doctor (Polkovyi Kvartermistr, Auditor i Lekar')*—were exactly like those for non-combatants in Cuirassier and Dragoon regiments (138).

In regard to colors, Hussar regiments had the following **distinctions**:

In the Pavlograd Regiment:

For lower ranks—sky-blue pelisse with black fur trim and yellow cords and buttons; dark-green dolman with sky-blue collar and cuffs, yellow cords, and white buttons; dark-green bag on the headdress, while cords and tassels were yellow with sky blue; sky-blue sash with yellow bindings and tassels; the top of the *sabertache* was dark green with yellow monogram, crown, and smooth trim, and with yellow and sky-blue cord; white saddle cloth with dark-green trim and the same cord, monograms, and crowns as on the sabertache; brass mountings on the saber scabbard (Illus. 1047). *For officers*—grey fur trim on the pelisse; all cords and buttons gold; eagles on the saddle cloth of dark-green cloth (Illus. 1047)(139). This regiment was the only one whose uniform greatly diverged from the general rules for hussar clothing.

In the Sumy Regiment:

For lower ranks—sky-blue pelisse; straw-colored dolman with sky-blue collar and cuffs; straw-colored bag on the headdress; all cords and buttons white: sky-blue sash with white bindings and tassels; sky-blue sabertache and saddle cloth, with smooth white trim and monograms (Illus. 1050). *For officers*—silver appointments; gold cord and eagle on the saddle cloth (140).

In the Mariupol Regiment:

For lower ranks—blue (*sinii*) pelisse; white dolman with straw-colored collar and cuffs; white bag on the headdress; all cords and buttons yellow; yellow sash with red bindings and tassels; straw-colored sabertache with smooth white trim and monogram (Illus. 1051); blue saddle cloth with straw-colored trim and yellow monograms. *For officers*—gold appointments, cords, and eagle on the saddle cloth (141).

In the Aleksandriya Regiment:

For lower ranks—black pelisse; black dolman with red collar and cuffs; black bag on the headdress; all cords and buttons white; white sash with red bindings and tassels; black sabertache with toothed red trim and monogram; black saddle cloth with white trim and monograms (Illus. 1052);. *For officers*—silver appointments; gold cords, and monogram on the saddle cloth (142).

In the Izyum Regiment:

For lower ranks—dark-blue (*temnosinii*) pelisse; crimson (*alyi*) dolman with dark-blue collar and cuffs; crimson bag on the headdress; all cords and buttons white; dark-blue sash with white bindings and tassels; crimson sabertache with smooth white trim and monogram; dark-blue saddle cloth with crimson trim and white cord and monograms (Illus. 1053);. *For officers*—gold appointments; yellow boots; gold cord and eagles on the saddle cloth (Illus. 1053) (143).

In the Akhtyrka Regiment:

For lower ranks—brown (*korichnevyi*) pelisse with straw-colored collar and cuffs (i.e. on the dolman – M.C.); brown bag on the headdress; cords and buttons yellow; yellow sash with white bindings and tassels; brown sabertache with toothed straw-colored trim and yellow monogram (Illus. 1055); brown saddle cloth with straw-colored trim and yellow monograms. *For officers*—gold appointments (Illus. 1055); gold cord and eagles on the saddle cloth (144).

In the Yelisavetgrad Regiment:

For lower ranks—straw-colored pelisse; straw-colored dolman with red collar and cuffs; straw-colored bag on the headdress; cords and buttons yellow; red sash with white bindings and tassels; straw-colored sabertache with orange toothed trim and monogram (Illus. 1056); red saddle cloth with orange trim and yellow cord and monograms. *For officers*—gold appointments; gold cord and eagles on the saddle cloth (145).

In the Olviopol Regiment:

For lower ranks—dark-green pelisse; dolman, and bag on the headdress; cords and buttons white; red sash with white bindings and tassels; dark-green sabertache with white toothed trim and monogram (Illus. 1056); dark-green saddle cloth with white trim and monograms. *For officers*—silever appointments; silver cord on the saddle cloth; gold eagles on the saddle cloth corners (146).

5 January 1798 – The *stable master* and *wagon master* (*shtalmeister i vagenmeister*) introduced into the organizational table for Hussar regiments were prescribed uniforms; for the first—as for stable masters in Cuirassier and Dragoon regiments (147), and for the second—as for hussar non-commissioned offices (148). Along with this, the price for hussar horses was established to be 40 roubles (149).

8 Febuary 1798 – Lower ranks in the *Pavlograd Hussar Regiment* were ordered to have white cords and tassels throughout instead of yellow; buttons were to be yellow, and the saddle cloth light turquoise (*svetlo-biryuzovyi*), with yellow trim and cord and white monograms. Officers were given the same saddle cloths except with gold cord and eagles (150).

20 August 1798 – *General Major Chorba's Hussar Regiment*, established on this date, was given uniforms as follows: *for lower ranks*—raspberry pelisse, dolman, and bag on the headdress; all cords and buttons white; raspberry sash with white bindings and tassels; raspberry sabertache and saddle cloth, with white trim and monograms (Illus. 1058). *For officers*—silver apppointments and cord on the saddle cloth; gold eagles on the saddle cloth corners (Illus. 1058) (151).

31 January 1799 – The hussars' cloaks were replaced by *greatcoats* of the same pattern as those for cuirassiers and dragoons (152).

9 October 1799 – Hussar officers were ordered to have raspberry silk on their **sword knots** and **sashes** in addition to the black and orange silk (153).

2 March 1800 – The *Aleksandriya Hussar Regiment* was given the uniform of Gotovitskii's disbanded regiment, formerly Chorba's (Illus. 1058) (154).

31 March 1800 – The two *Moscow Hussar Squadrons* joined to the Akhtyrka Hussar Regiment were ordered to wear the uniform of that regiment (155).

NOTES

(11) Pattern and various other cuirassier uniform clothing items from that time preserved by the Commissariat Department of the War Ministry (now the Main Intendance Administration (*Glavnoe Intendantskoe Upravlenie*), in the pattern storehouse of this Administration's Technical Committee) and in HIS IMPERIAL HIGHNESS GRAND DUKE MICHAEL PAVLOVICH'S Own Arsenal; drawings located in HIS IMPERIAL MAJESTY'S Own Library under No. 177; Military Regulation for Cavalry Service, 29 November 1796, Chapter LXXVI; HIGHEST confirmed table of uniforms, accouterments, and weaponry for a Cuirassier regiment, 5 January 1798, and statements by contemporaries.

(2) Ditto.

(3) Ditto.

(4) Ditto.

(5) Ditto.

(6) Ditto.

(7) Ditto.

(8) Ditto.

(9) Ditto.

(10) Ditto.

(11) Ditto.

(12) Ditto.

(13) The table referenced in the preceding note; the description of uniforms for Cuirassier and Dragoon regiments confirmed by HIGHEST Authority and an announcement to the Commissariat in February 1797, and a broad sword from those preserved in the St.-Petersburg Arsenal.

(14) The table and description of uniforms referenced in the preceding note; Military Regulation for Cavalry Service, 29 November 1796, Chapter LXXVI, § 4, and model sword knot and sword belt preserved in the Commissariat Department of the War Ministry.

(15) Ditto.

(16) Ditto.

(17) The same table; Military Regulation, 29 November 1796, Chapter LXXVI, note to § 4, and model pattern sabertache, girdle, and cuirass preserved in the Commissariat Department of the War Ministry.

(18) Ditto.

(19) The same table and a pattern carbine preserved in the St.-Petersburg Arsenal.

(20) The same table; Military Regulation of 29 November 1796, Chapter LXXVI, §§ 9 and 13, and cuirassier shoulder belts and pouches from that time preserved in the personal arsenals of HIS IMPERIAL AND SOVEREIGN MAJESTY and HISIMPERIALHIGHNESSGRANDDUKEMICHAEL PAVLOVICH.

(21) Ditto.

(22) The same table and a pistol from those preserved in the St.-Petersburg Arsenal.

(23) The same table; Military Regulation of 29 November 1796, Chapter LXXVI, §§ 11 and 17; the description of uniforms referenced above in Note 13; actual model items preserved in the Commissariat Department of the War Ministry.

(24) Ditto.

(25) Ditto.

(26) Ditto.

(27) The same table and the Military Regulation of 29 November 1796, Chapter LXXVI, § 5.

(28) Ditto.

(29) Ditto.

(30) Ditto.

(31) Ditto.

(32) Ditto.

(33) The same table; Military Regulation of 29 November 1796, Chapter LXXVI, § 15, and pattern uniform for a cuirassier trumpeter, preserved in the Commissariat Department of the War Ministry.

(34) The same table and the Military Regulation of 29 November 1796, Chapter LXXVI, § 25.

(35) The description of uniforms referenced in Note 13; *Chronicle of the Russian Imperial Army*, compiled by Prince Dolgorukov, Nos. 162-166; these same numbers in the collection of drawings located in HIS IMPERIAL MAJESTY'S Own Library under No. 177; uniform items and weapons of Cuirassier officers from that time, preserved in HISIMPERIALHIGHNESSGRANDDUKEMICHAEL PAVLOVICH'S Arsenal; Military Regulation for Cavalry Service, 29 November 1796, Chapter LXXVI, § 1, and statements by contemporaries.

(36) Ditto.

(37) Ditto.

(38) The description of uniforms referenced in Note 13; the Military Regulation of 29 November 1796, Chapter LXXVI, § 4, and statements by contemporaries.

(39) Drawings located in HIS IMPERIAL MAJESTY'S Own Library under No. 177, and statements by contemporaries.

(40) HIGHEST confirmed table of uniforms, accouterments, and weapons for a Cuirassier regiment, 5 January 1798, and statements by contemporaries.

(41) The description of uniforms referenced in Note 13, and statements by contemporaries.

(42) The same description of uniforms; *Chronicle of the Russian Imperial Army*, compiled by Prince Dolgorukov, No. 162, and this same number in the drawings located in HIS IMPERIAL MAJESTY'S Own Library under No. 177.

(43) Ibid., No. 163.

(44) Ibid., No. 164.

(45) Ibid., No. 165.

(46) Ibid., No. 166.

(47) Ibid., No. 167.

(48) Ibid., No. 168.

(49) Ibid., No. 169.

(50) Ibid., No. 170.

(51) Ibid., No. 171.

(52) Ibid., No. 172.

(53) Ibid., No. 173.

(54) Ibid., No. 174.

(55) Ibid., No. 175.

(56) Ibid., No. 176.

(57) Ibid., No. 177.

(58) HIGHEST confirmed table of uniforms, accouterments, and weapons for a Cuirassier regiment, 5 January 1798.

(59) *Chronicle of the Russian Imperial Army*, compiled by Prince Dolgorukov, No. 197, and this same number in the drawings located in HIS IMPERIAL MAJESTY'S Own Library under No. 177.

(60) Ibid., No. 196.

(61) Ibid., No. 198.

(62) HIGHEST Order and contemporary drawings, and actual items with such stars found in HISIMPERIALHIGHNESSGRANDDUKEMICHAEL PAVLOVICH'S Own Arsenal.

(63) Complete Collection of Laws of the Russian Empire (*Polnoe Sobranie Zakonov Rossiiskoi Imperii*, hereafter PSZ), Vol. XXIV, No 18,837, pg. 548, and statements by contemporaries.

(64) PSZ, Vol. XLIV, Part II, Sect. Four, under information on uniforms page 3, No. 19,178, and statements by

contemporaries.

(65) *Istoriya Leib-Gvardii Kirasirskago EGO IMPERATORSKAGO VELICHESTVA polka*, St. Petersburg, 1833. Page 19 and Note 9.

(66) The description of uniforms referenced in Note 13; pattern and various other dragoon uniform clothing items from that time preserved by the Commissariat Department of the War Ministry and in HIS IMPERIAL HIGHNESS GRAND DUKE MICHAEL PAVLOVICH'S Own Arsenal; drawings located in HIS IMPERIAL MAJESTY'S Own Library under No. 177; Military Regulation for Cavalry Service, 29 November 1796, Chapters LXXVI and Chapter LXXIX, § 2; HIGHEST confirmed table of uniforms, accouterments, and weaponry for a Dragoon regiment, 5 January 1798, and statements by contemporaries.

(67) Ditto.

(68) Ditto.

(69) Ditto.

(70) Ditto.

(71) Ditto.

(72) Ditto.

(73) Ditto.

(74) Ditto.

(75) Ditto.

(76) Ditto.

(77) The same sources as indicated in the previous notes 66-76 except for the table of 5 January 1798, which related only to lower ranks.

(78) Ditto.

(79) The same sources as indicated in Notes 66-76.

(80) The description of uniforms reference in Note 13, and statements by contemporaries.

(81) The same description of uniforms; *Chronicle of the Russian Imperial Army*, compiled by Prince Dolgorukov, No. 178, and this same number in the drawings located in HIS IMPERIAL MAJESTY'S Own Library under No. 177.

(82) Ditto, No. 179.

(83) The same description of uniforms.

(84) The same description of uniforms; *Chronicle of the Russian Imperial Army*, compiled by Prince Dolgorukov, No. 181, and this same number in the drawings located in HIS IMPERIAL MAJESTY'S Own Library under No. 177.

(85) Ditto, No. 182.

(86) Ditto, No. 183.

(87) Ditto, No. 184.

(88) Ditto, No. 185.

(89) Ditto, No. 186.

(90) Ditto, No. 187.

(91) Ditto, No. 188.

(92) Ditto, No. 189.

(93) Ditto, No. 190.

(94) Ditto, No. 191.

(95) Ditto, No. 192.

(96) Ditto, No. 193.

(97) HIGHEST confirmed table of uniforms, accouterments, and weapons for a Dragoon regiment, 5 January 1798.

(98) HIGHEST Directive to the Military Collegium; *Chronicle of the Russian Imperial Army*, compiled by Prince Dolgorukov, No. 180, and this same number in the drawings located in HIS IMPERIAL MAJESTY'S Own

Library under No. 177.

(99) In the same *Chronicle* and drawings Nos. 199 and 200.

(100) Ditto.

(101) PSZ XXV, No. 18,837, pg. 548, and statements from contemporaries.

(102) PSZ XLIV, Part II, sect. four, under information for uniforms, page 3, No. 19,178, and statements by contemporaries.

(103) HIGHEST Order.

(104) HIGHEST Order.

(105) HIGHEST Order.

(106) Pattern and various other hussar uniform clothing items from that time preserved by the Commissariat Department of the War Ministry and in HIS IMPERIAL HIGHNESS GRAND DUKE MICHAEL PAVLOVICH'S Arsenal; drawings located in HIS IMPERIAL MAJESTY'S Own Library under No. 177; HIGHEST confirmed table of uniforms, accouterments, and weaponry for a Hussar regiment, 5 January 1798, and statements by contemporaries.

(107) Ditto.

(108) Ditto.

(109) Ditto.

(110) Ditto.

(111) Ditto.

(112) Ditto.

(113) Ditto.

(114) The table referenced in the preceding note.

(115) The same table and a model hussar saber preserved in the St.-Petersburg Arsenal.

(116) The same table and a pattern sword knot preserved by the Commissariat Department of the War Ministry.

(117) The same table and contemporary hussar sword belts preserved in various arsenals and by private persons.

(118) The same table; sabertaches preserved in HIS IMPERIAL HIGHNESS GRAND DUKE MICHAEL PAVLOVICH'S Own Arsenal, and various drawings of contemporary hussar uniforms, including those in HIS IMPERIAL MAJESTY'S Own Library under No. 177.

(119) The same table and a pattern barrel sash preserved by the Commissariat Department of the War Ministry.

(120) The same table and a carbine from those preserved in the St.-Petersburg Arsenal.

(121) The same table.

(122) The same table and a cartridge pouch preserved by the Commissariat Department of the War Ministry.

(123) The same table and a pistol from those preserved in the St.-Petersburg Arsenal.

(124) The same table.

(125) The same table; a pattern saddle cloth preserved by the Commissariat Department of the War Ministry, and drawings in HIS IMPERIAL MAJESTY'S Own Library under No. 177.

(126) The same table.

(127) Ditto.

(128) Ditto.

(129) Military Regulation for Cavalry Service, 29 November 1796, Chapter LXXVII, § 5.

(130) HIGHEST confirmed table of uniforms, accouterments, and weaponry for a Hussar regiment, 5 January 1798, and statements from contemporaries.

(131) Ditto.

(132) Ditto.

(133) Ditto.

(134) Actual items that were part of hussar officers' uniforms and horse furniture at that time, preserved in various arsenals and by private persons; various contemporary drawings, including those in HIS IMPERIAL MAJESTY'S Own Library under No. 177, and statements by contemporaries.

(135) Statements by contemporaries and various contemporary drawings.

(136) Ditto.

(137) Ditto.

(138) HIGHEST confirmed table of uniforms, accouterments, and weaponry for a Hussar regiment, 5 January 1798, and statements from contemporaries.

(139) HIGHEST confirmed description of the uniform for Major General Baur's (Pavlograd) Hussar Regiment, 29 November 1798, preserved in the Archive of the Commissariat Department of the War Ministry.

(140) *Chronicle of the Russian Imperial Army*, compiled by Prince Dolgorukov, and in its associated drawings preserved in HIS IMPERIAL MAJESTY'S Own Library under No. 177, No. 247.

(141) Ditto, No. 251.

(142) Ditto, No. 250.

(143) Ditto, No. 249.

(144) Ditto, No. 248.

(145) Ditto, No. 253.

(146) Ditto, No. 254.

(147) Statements by contemporaries.

(148) HIGHEST confirmed table of uniforms, accouterments, and weaponry for a Hussar regiment, 5 January 1798.

(149) Ibid.

(150) HIGHEST Directive to the Military Collegium, 8 February 1798, preserved in the Archive of the Commissariat Department of the War Ministry.

(151) *Chronicle of the Russian Imperial Army*, compiled by Prince Dolgorukov, No. 255, and in the collection of drawings located in HIS IMPERIAL MAJESTY'S Own Library under No. 159, between leaves 60 and 61.

(152) PSZ, XXV, No. 18,837, pg. 548.

(153) PSZ, XLIV, Part II, sect. four, under information for uniforms, page 3, No. 19,178, and statements by contemporaries.

(154) HIGHEST Directive preserved in the files of the Archive of the Commissariat Department of the War Ministry.

(155) HIGHEST Order.

РИСУНКИ
Одежды и Вооруженія
РОССІЙСКИХЪ
ВОЙСКЪ.

PLATES LIST OF ILLUSTRATIONS

First plate: **Paul I** , Russia Emperor between 1796 and 1801.

1017 and 1018. Private and Officer. HIS MAJESTY'S Cuirassier Regiment, 1797-1801.

1019. Privates. HER MAJESTY'S Cuirassier Regiment, 1797-1801.

1020. Officer and Private. HER MAJESTY'S Cuirassier Regiment, 1797-1801.

1021. Cuirassiers. HER MAJESTY'S Cuirassier Regiment, 1797-1801. (In smocks (*V kitelyakh*).)

1022. Cuirassier weapons and accouterments, 1796-1801. a. Cuirass; b. Girdle; c. Sword belt with broadsword and sabertache; d. Sword knot; e. Carbine; f. Shoulder belt; g. Cartridge pouch; and h. Pistol.

1023. Officer and Non-commissioned Officer. Military Order Cuirassier Regiment, 1797-1801.

1024. Distinguished Officer Candidate (*Estandart-Yunker*) of the Yekaterinoslav Cuirassier Regiment, and Trumpeter of the Kazan Cuirassier Regiment, 1797-1801.

1025. Staff-Trumpeters. Ryazan and Yamburg Cuirassier Regiments, 1797-1800, and Glukhov Cuirassier Regiment, 1797-1801.

1026. Kettledrummers. Kiev (1797-1801) and Nezhin (1797-1800) Cuirassier Regiments.

1027. Officers. Sofiya Cuirassier Regiment, 1797-1800, and Starodub Cuirassier Regiment, 1797-1801.

1028. Officer, Riga Cuirassier Regiment, and Non-commissioned Officer, Chernigov Cuirassier Regiment, 1797-1801.

1029. Cuirass and Broadsword for Cuirassier Officers, 1797-1801.

1030. Generals. Kharkov and Little-Russia Cuirassier Regiments, 1797-1801. (In undress coats (*vitse-mundiry*).)

1031. Stable Master. Cuirassier regiment, 1797-1800.

1032. Privates. Neplyuev's and Friderici's Cuirassier Regiments (1798-1800), and Zorn's Cuirassier Regiment (1798-1801).

1033. Star for sabertaches, shabracks, and pistol holders of the HER MAJESTY'S Leib-Cuirassier Regiment, awarded 8 October 1798.

1034. Private and Officer. Vladimir Dragoon Regiment, 1797-1801.

1035. Musket and Broadsword for Dragoon Regiments, 1797-1801.

1036. Officer and Non-commissioned Officer. AstrakhanDragoon Regiment, 1797-1800.

1037. Dinstinguished Officer Candidate (*Fanen-Yunker*). Nizhnii-Novgorod Dragoon Regiment, 1797-1800.

1038. Drummer. Pskov Dragoon Regiment, 1797-1801.

1039. Trumpeter, Smolensk Dragoon Regiment, and Officer, St.-Petersburg Dragoon Regiment, 1797-1801.

1040. Staff-Trumpeter. Taganrog Dragoon Regiment, 1797-1800.

1041. Officer and Hautboy Players. Irkutsk Dragoon Regiment, 1797-1800.

1042. Kettledrummers. Siberia, Orenburg, and Ingermanland Dragoon Regiments, 1797-1801.

1043. Officers. Narva and Rostov Dragoon Regiments, 1797-1800.

1044. Officer. Moscow Dragoon Regiment, 1797-1800.

1045. General, Kargopol Dragoon Regiment, and Officer, Seversk Dragoon Regiment, 1797-1801.

1046. Non-commissioned Officer, Schreiders' Dragoon Regiment, 1797-1801, and Private, Khastatov's Dragoon Regiment, 1797-1800.

1047. Private and Officer. Pavlograd Hussar Regiment, 1797-1798.

1048. Hussar headdress, 1797-1801.

1049. Barrel-sash, Sword Belt with Saber and Sabertache, and Carbine. Pistol, Shabrack, and Cartridge Pouch. Hussar Regiments, 1797-1801.

1050. Non-commissioned Officer. Sumy Hussar Regiment, 1797-1801.

1051. Trumpeter. Mariupol Hussar Regiment, 1797-1801.

1052. Staff-Trumpeter. Aleksandriya Hussar Regiment, 1797-1800.

1053. Officer and Non-commissioned Officer. Izyum Hussar Regiment, 1797-1801.

1054. Shabrack and Sabertache for Hussar Officers, 1797-1801.

1055. Non-commissioned Officer and Officer (in undress coat (*vengerka*)). Akhtyrka Hussar Regiment, 1797-1801.

1056 and 1057. General, Yelisavetgrad Hussar Regiment, and Trumpeter, Olviopol Hussar Regiment, 1797-1801.

1058. Officer and Private. Chorba's Hussar Regiment, 1798-1801.

Рисовалъ Теребеневъ.

Рис на камнъ Смирновъ.

Paul I, Russia Emperor between 1796 and 1801.

Private and Officer. HIS MAJESTY'S Cuirassier Regiment, 1797-1801.

Privates. HER MAJESTY'S Cuirassier Regiment, 1797-1801.

Officer and Private. HER MAJESTY'S Cuirassier Regiment, 1797-1801.

Cuirassiers. HER MAJESTY'S Cuirassier Regiment, 1797-1801.

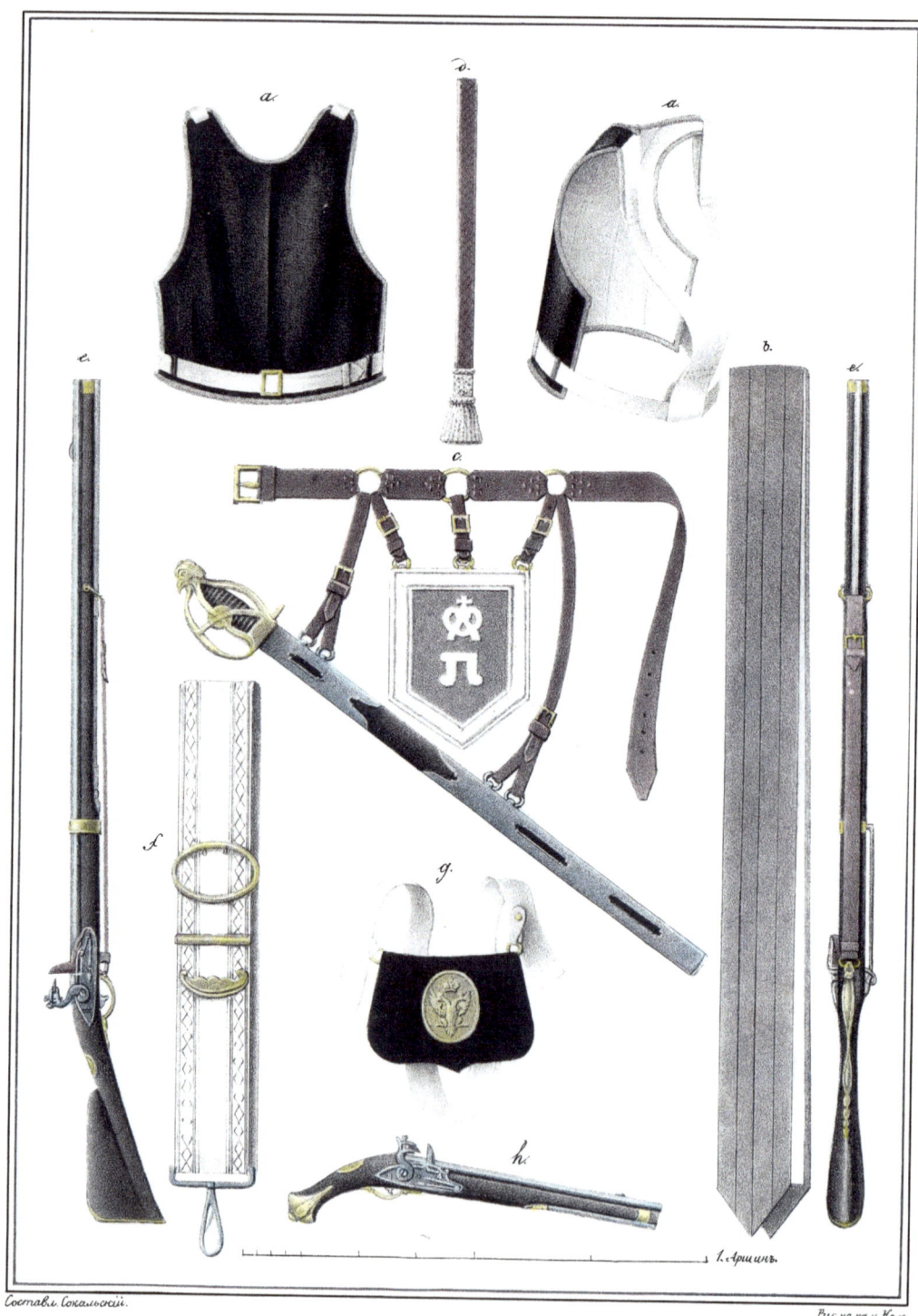

Cuirassier weapons and accouterments, 1796-1801. a. Cuirass; b. Girdle; c. Sword belt with broadsword and sabertache; d. Sword knot; e. Carbine; f. Shoulder belt; g. Cartridge pouch; and h. Pistol.

Officer and Non-commissioned Officer. Military Order Cuirassier Regiment, 1797-1801.

Distinguished Officer Candidate (Estandart-Yunker) of the Yekaterinoslav Cuirassier Regiment, and Trumpeter of the Kazan Cuirassier Regiment, 1797-1801.

Staff-Trumpeters. Ryazan and Yamburg Cuirassier Regiments, 1797-1800,
and Glukhov Cuirassier Regiment, 1797-1801.

Kettledrummers. Kiev (1797-1801) and Nezhin (1797-1800) Cuirassier Regiments.

Officers. Sofiya Cuirassier Regiment, 1797-1800, and Starodub Cuirassier Reg., 1797-1801.

Officer, Riga Cuirassier Regiment, and Non-commissioned Officer,
Chernigov Cuirassier Regiment, 1797-1801.

Cuirass and Broadsword for Cuirassier Officers, 1797-1801.

1030.

Generals. Kharkov and Little-Russia Cuirassier Regiments, 1797-1801. (In undress coat)

Stable Master. Cuirassier regiment, 1797-1800.

Privates. Neplyuev's and Friderici's Cuirassier Regiments (1798-1800),
and Zorn's Cuirassier Regiment (1798-1801).

Star for sabertaches, shabracks, and pistol holders of the HER MAJESTY'S Leib-Cuirassier Regiment, awarded 8 October 1798.

Составил Пиратскій и Губаревъ.   Рис. на кам. Жарковъ.

Private and Officer. Vladimir Dragoon Regiment, 1797-1801.

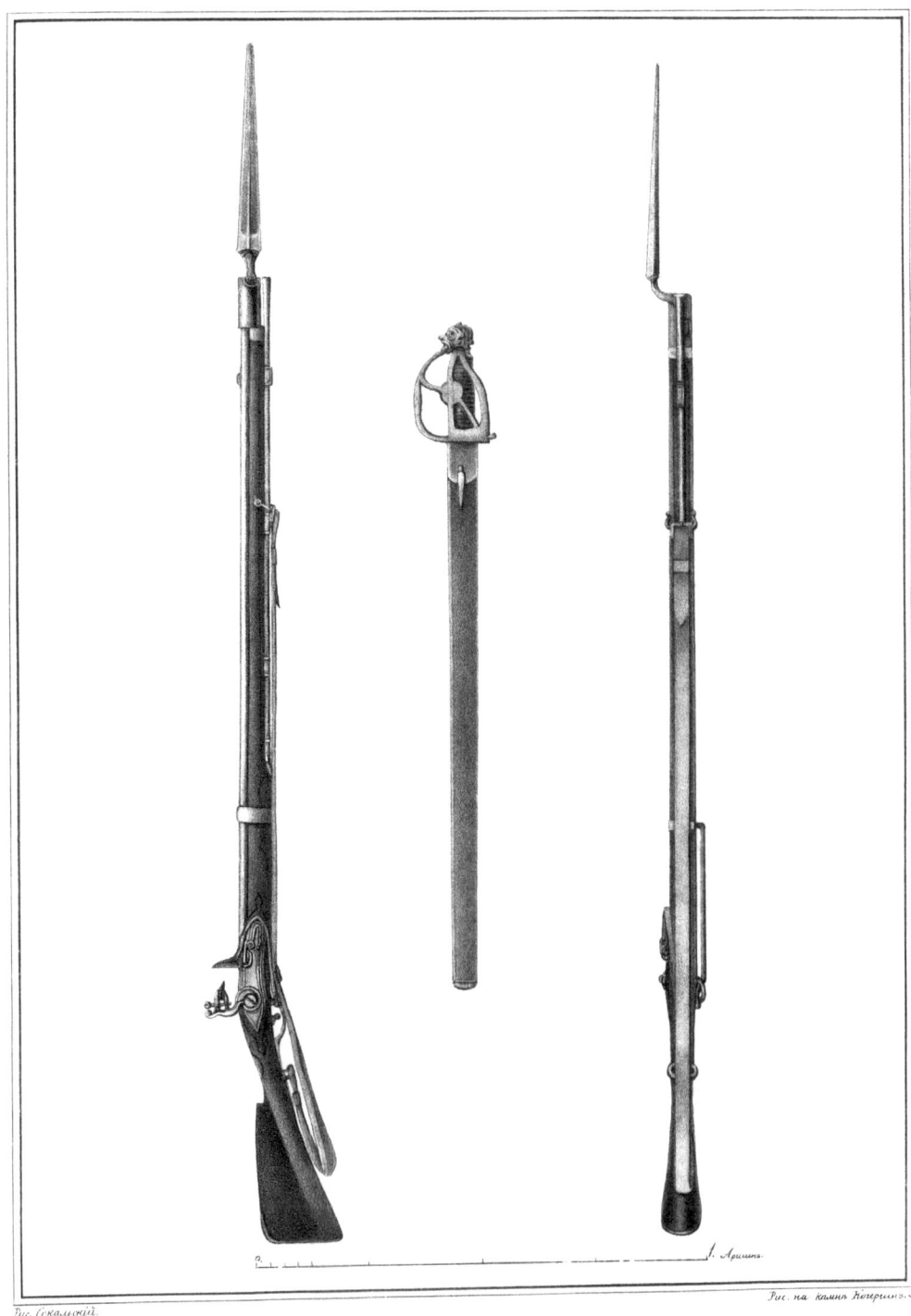

Musket and Broadsword for Dragoon Regiments, 1797-1801.

Officer and Non-commissioned Officer. AstrakhanDragoon Regiment, 1797-1800.

Dinstinguished Officer Candidate (Fanen-Yunker). Nizhnii-Novgorod
Dragoon Regiment, 1797-1800.

1038.

Drummer. Pskov Dragoon Regiment, 1797-1801.

Trumpeter, Smolensk Dragoon Regiment, and Officer, St.-Petersburg
Dragoon Regiment, 1797-1801.

1040.

Составл: Ниратскій и Губаревъ. Рис. на кам. Гиллерз

Staff-Trumpeter. Taganrog Dragoon Regiment, 1797-1800.

Составл. Губаревъ и Разумихинъ.   Рис. на кам. Белоусовъ и Петровскій.

Officer and Hautboy Players. Irkutsk Dragoon Regiment, 1797-1800.

1042.

Kettledrummers. Siberia, Orenburg, and Ingermanland Dragoon Regiments, 1797-1801.

Составл. Губаревъ и Разумихинъ.   Рис. на кам. Бѣлоусовъ и Гиллеръ.

Officers. Narva and Rostov Dragoon Regiments, 1797-1800.

Составъ Пиратскій и Губаревъ.

Рис. на кам. Шмицъ.

Officer. Moscow Dragoon Regiment, 1797-1800.

General, Kargopol Dragoon Regiment, and Officer, Seversk Dragoon Regiment, 1797-1801.

1846.

Non-commissioned Officer, Schreiders' Dragoon Regiment, 1797-1801,
and Private, Khastatov's Dragoon Regiment, 1797-1800.

1047.

Private and Officer. Pavlograd Hussar Regiment, 1797-1798.

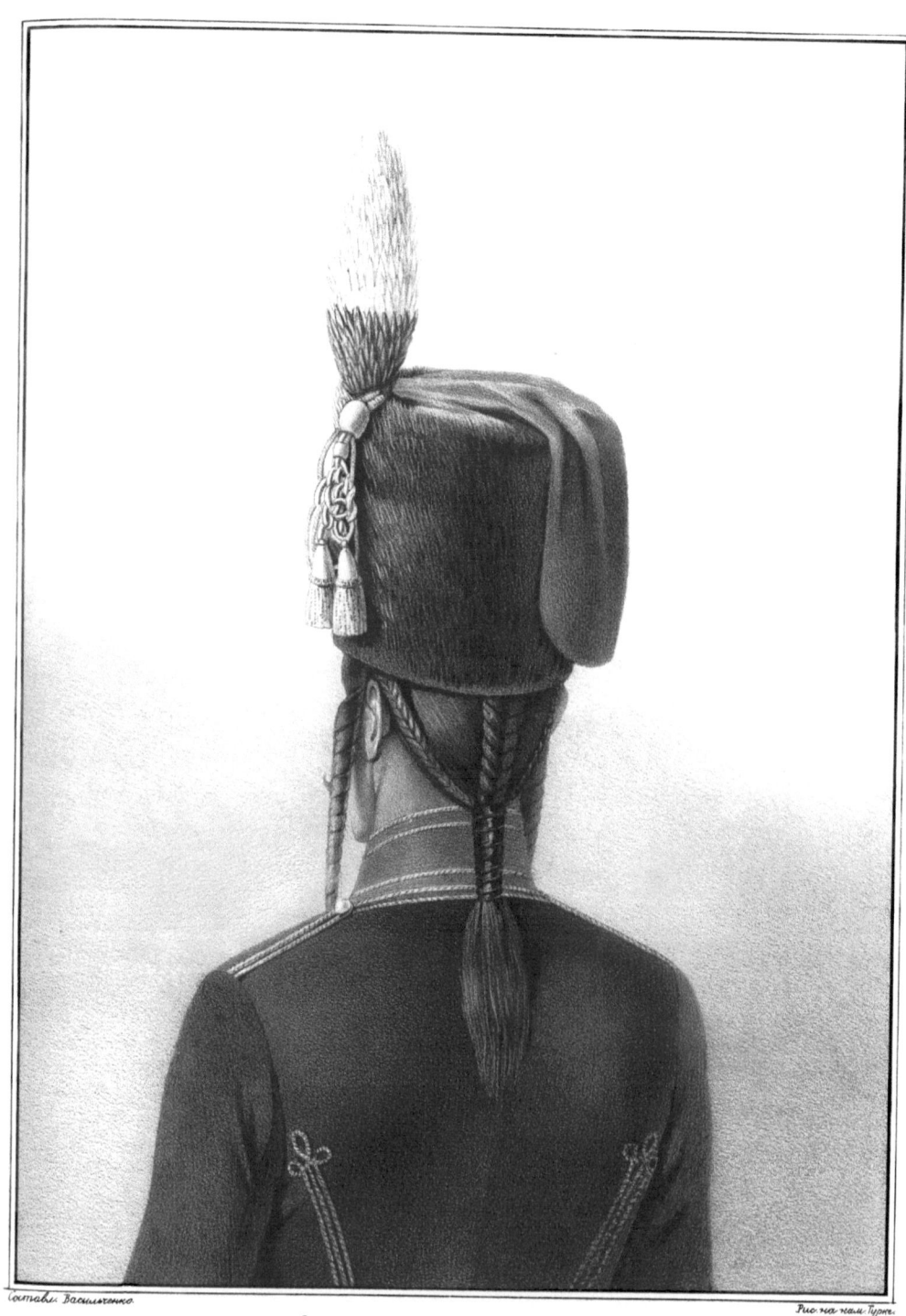

Составил Васильченко.   Рис. на кам. Пурке.

Hussar headdress, 1797-1801.

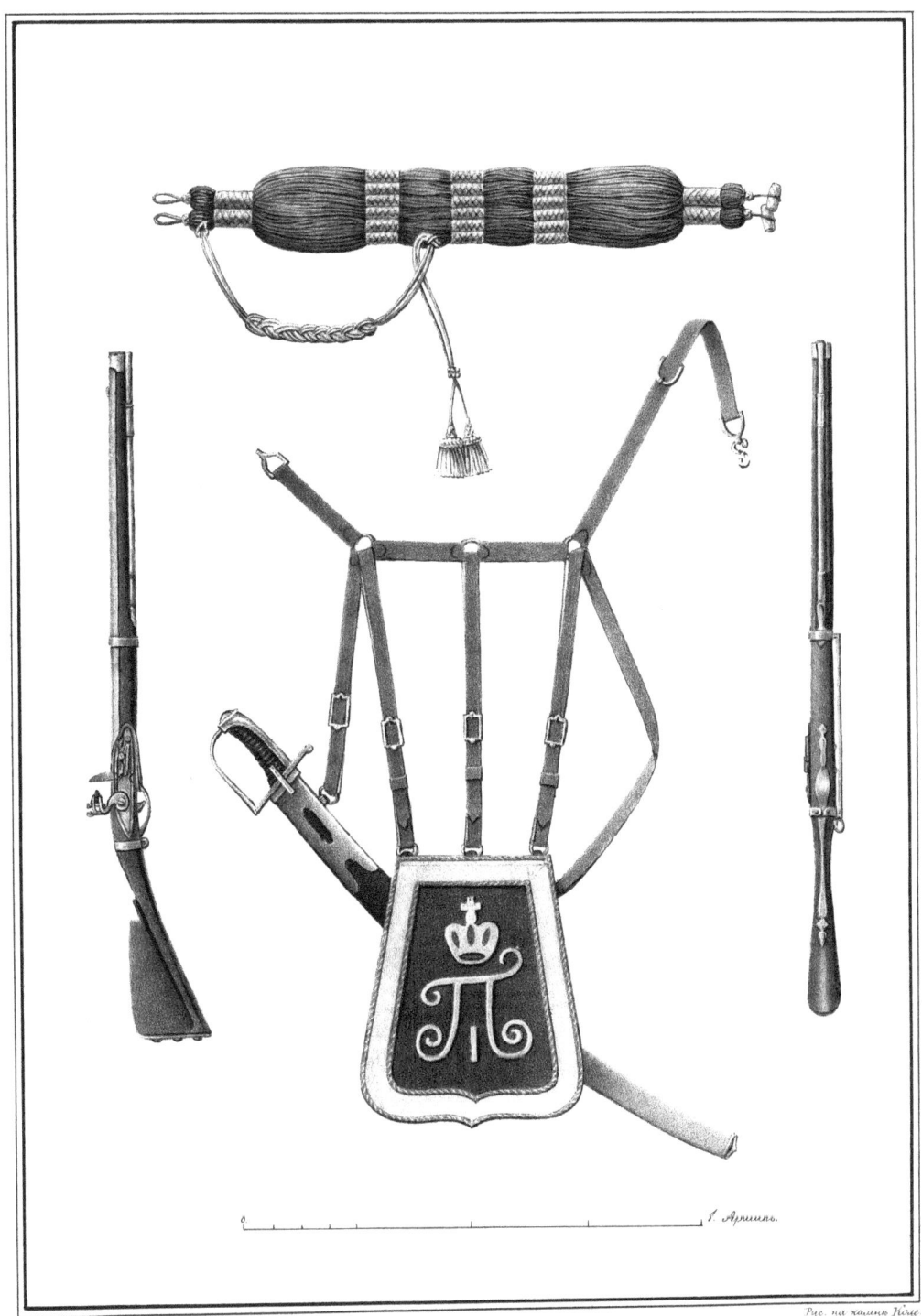

Barrel-sash, Sword Belt with Saber and Sabertache, and Carbine. Pistol, Shabrack, and Cartridge Pouch. Hussar Regiments, 1797-1801.

1050.

Non-commissioned Officer. Sumy Hussar Regiment, 1797-1801.

Trumpeter. Mariupol Hussar Regiment, 1797-1801.

Составъ: Губаревъ и Клюкѣинъ.

Рис: на кам: Бѣлоуровъ и Марковъ.

Staff-Trumpeter. Aleksandriya Hussar Regiment, 1797-1800.

Officer and Non-commissioned Officer. Izyum Hussar Regiment, 1797-1801.

Составл. Сокольский.

Рис. на кам. Кочерин.

Shabrack and Sabertache for Hussar Officers, 1797-1801.

1055.

Non-commissioned Officer and Officer (in undress coat (vengerka)).
Akhtyrka Hussar Regiment, 1797-1801.

General, Yelisavetgrad Hussar Regiment, and Trumpeter,
Olviopol Hussar Regiment, 1797-1801.

Рис. Сокольский. *Рис. на камнѣ Коли.*

Plum particular of General, Yelisavetgrad Hussar Regiment, 1797-1801.

Officer and Private. Chorba's Hussar Regiment, 1798-1801.

WORK PLAN

Our reprint in based on the original 19th century volumes, to be precise the volumes from 7 to 9 are dedicated to the reign of Paul I; this first part is distributed on 7 volumes, having a numbering from 1 to 7. From number 10 to 18 of the original volumes, the second part is dedicated to the Russian troops under Alexander I. These still being worked on and they will be soon ready, distributed on twenty volumes approximately. Our new edition, the first ever published in English, both on paper and digital format, boasts a large number of color plates, many of them unpublished and coloured by our team of expert artists and scholars of uniformology. Each volume is based on 50/70 plates, always accompanied by the original translated text which describes the uniforms, the organization and the armament of the Russian army of the period.

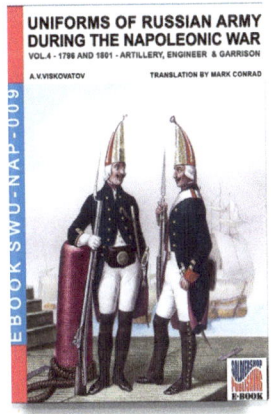 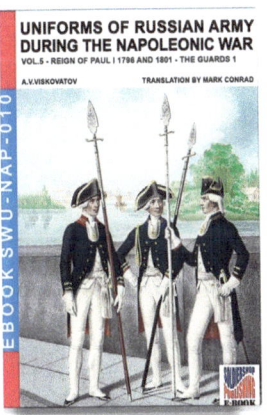